Prayers of Easter: A Journey of Faith, Hope, and Renewal

A 40-Day Devotional with Family Prayers, Easter Reflections, and Resurrection Hope

Karen Kazimer Shockley

Karen's Words

Prayers of Easter: A Journey of Faith, Hope, and Renewal

Prayers of Easter is a beautifully crafted spiritual companion for the Lenten and Easter season, designed to draw readers closer to the heart of Christ through Scripture, reflection, and prayer. Whether used for personal devotion, family worship, or church settings, this book gently leads believers through the sorrow of the cross into the joy of the resurrection—and beyond.

WHAT'S INSIDE

Section 1: Preparing for Easter – Lent and Holy Week Prayers

A week-by-week guide through Ash Wednesday, the Lenten journey, and each day of Holy Week, including Palm Sunday, Maundy Thursday, Good Friday, and Holy Saturday. Each day features a heartfelt prayer and Scripture to lead the reader through repentance, reflection, and renewal.

Section 2: Resurrection Prayers

Joyful prayers celebrating Easter Sunday and the miracle of the empty tomb. These devotions focus on spiritual rebirth, thanksgiving, and living in the power of Christ's resurrection.

Section 3: Easter Week & the Season of Resurrection

Explores the weeks following Easter Sunday, encouraging readers to carry the light of resurrection into everyday life. Includes prayers for courage, sharing the Gospel, peace, family, and spiritual growth.

Section 4: Easter Reflections and Blessings

Morning and evening blessings, spiritual reflections, and prayers for transitions throughout the day. Designed to help readers remain grounded in Easter hope no matter the season or circumstance.

Section 5: Weekly Devotions

Weekly Devotional Reflections for Lent and Easter to accompany and deepen your prayer journey.

Section 6: Family and Children's Prayers

Simple, heartfelt prayers to guide your family's Easter season. The Easter story is for everyone—including the youngest hearts in our homes. This section offers short prayers and blessings written especially for children and families. Whether shared at the breakfast table, before bed, or during family devotions, these prayers invite children to celebrate the joy of Jesus' resurrection and feel God's love for them.

Section 7: Easter Blessings for Special Occasions

The resurrection of Jesus fills every corner of our lives with meaning—from quiet moments of personal faith to the joyful celebrations shared around a table or in a sanctuary. These blessings are crafted for special occasions during the Easter season. Use them at home, in church, or wherever hearts gather in the light of Christ's victory.

Section 8: Personal Testimonies and Stories

Features short, powerful testimonies from women, children, and others who experienced resurrection hope in their lives. These real-life reflections make the Easter message personal and relatable.

Section 9: Easter Symbols, Traditions & Reflections

A look at the deeper meanings behind Easter imagery like the cross, the empty tomb, lilies, the lamb, and more—paired with Scripture and reflection prompts. Also includes printable coloring pages for teaching and meditation.

Section 10: Family Devotions and Activities

Simple, creative devotions and interactive activities designed for families with children. Includes scripture, discussion questions, and hands-on ideas to build joyful Easter traditions at home.

Section 11: Journaling Pages & Reflection Prompts

Guided journaling prompts for each week of Lent and Easter, with space for readers to respond, write prayers, or record insights from their journey.

Bonus Resources:

- **Printable Check-Off Chart** for daily Easter Scripture readings
- **Prayer Cards for Children and Families**
- **Easter Blessings Cards** for special occasions
- **Illustrated Coloring Pages** focused on symbols of Easter

INTRODUCTION

Easter is the heart of the Christian faith—a celebration of Jesus Christ's resurrection, the victory over sin and death, and the promise of eternal life. It is more than just a holiday; it is a season of awe and transformation, of remembering the cross and rejoicing in the empty tomb. From the solemn reflection of Lent to the triumphant cries of "He is risen!" Easter invites believers to walk the path of Christ's passion and glory.

Prayer plays a vital role in this sacred journey. It draws us closer to God, opens our hearts to His voice, and allows us to participate in the mystery of redemption. In the Easter season, prayer becomes a bridge between sorrow and joy, between the cross and the crown. Through prayer, we remember Christ's sacrifice, celebrate His resurrection, and prepare our hearts to live as people of hope and resurrection power.

This book was created as a companion for your spiritual journey through Easter. Whether you are reading alone during quiet morning devotions, gathered around the table with your family, or leading a group in worship or church service, *Prayers of Easter* is designed to meet you where you are. Each prayer is meant to guide reflection, stir the heart, and deepen your connection to God through the lens of Easter.

You are encouraged to return to these prayers not just during Holy Week, but throughout the Easter season and beyond. May these words remind you of the unshakable hope we have in Christ and inspire you to live in the light of the resurrection every day.

SECTION 1: PREPARING

FOR EASTER

Section 1:
Preparing for Easter
Lent and Holy Week Prayers

The journey to **Easter** begins in the quiet shadow of **Lent**—a season marked by reflection, repentance, and renewal. It is a time when we turn our hearts inward, examine our lives in the light of Christ's sacrifice, and draw closer to the cross.

In these sacred days leading up to Easter, we walk with Jesus: through the desert of temptation, the streets of Jerusalem, the Upper Room, the Garden of Gethsemane, and ultimately, to Calvary.

In these sacred days leading up to Easter, we walk with Jesus: through the desert of temptation, the streets of Jerusalem, the Upper Room, the Garden of Gethsemane, and ultimately, to Calvary.

The journey to Easter begins in the quiet shadow of Lent—a season marked by reflection, repentance, and renewal. It is a time when we turn our hearts inward, examine our lives in the light of Christ's sacrifice, and draw closer to the cross. In these sacred days leading up to Easter, we walk with Jesus: through the desert of temptation, the streets of Jerusalem, the Upper Room, the Garden of Gethsemane, and ultimately, to Calvary.

This section offers prayers to guide your soul through Ash Wednesday, the weeks of Lent, and each holy day of Passion Week. Whether you are seeking forgiveness, longing for spiritual renewal, or preparing your heart to receive the risen Lord, these prayers are here to accompany you on the way. May they help you slow down, listen deeply, and embrace the hope that is coming.

ASH WEDNESDAY – A PRAYER FOR REPENTANCE AND RENEWAL

SCRIPTURE:

"Create in me a clean heart, O God; and renew a right spirit within me." – Psalm 51:10 (KJV)

PRAYER:

Lord God,

On this Ash Wednesday, I come before You with a humble heart. I confess my sins and lay them at the foot of the cross. I acknowledge my need for Your mercy, for I have fallen short in thought, word, and deed.

Wash me clean, O God. Mark this day as a turning point—a day when I choose renewal, repentance, and a return to You. Prepare my soul for the Lenten journey ahead. Help me walk with Christ, carrying my cross with grace.

In Jesus' name, Amen.

LENTEN DEVOTION – A PRAYER FOR SPIRITUAL GROWTH AND SACRIFICE

SCRIPTURE:

"Then said Jesus unto his disciples, If any man will come after me, let him deny himself, and take up his cross, and follow me." – Matthew 16:24 (KJV)

PRAYER:

Jesus,

As I journey through this season of Lent, teach me what it means to follow You more closely. Help me surrender the distractions and comforts that keep me from deeper devotion. May my fasting remind me of Your sacrifice. May my prayers rise like incense to Heaven.

Let these forty days be a time of growth, pruning, and transformation. I want to be more like You—obedient, compassionate, and full of grace. Shape me in Your image.

Amen.

SCRIPTURE:

"Blessed is he that cometh in the name of the Lord; Hosanna in the highest." – Matthew 21:9 (KJV)

PRAYER:

Hosanna!
Today, Lord Jesus, I lift my voice with the crowds that welcomed You into Jerusalem. I wave my palm in praise, proclaiming You as King of Kings and Lord of Lords.
Help me not only to praise You in celebration but to follow You in obedience—even when the road leads to the cross. Let my heart be a temple cleansed and ready to receive You.
Reign in me, now and always.
Amen.

HOLY MONDAY TO WEDNESDAY – PRAYERS OF PREP-ARATION AND REFLECTION ON JESUS' TEACHINGS

SCRIPTURE:

"He taught them many things..." – Mark 4:2 (KJV)

PRAYER FOR MONDAY:

Lord,
As I reflect on Your cleansing of the temple, cleanse my heart of anything unworthy. Make me a house of prayer, not distraction. Help me seek holiness, not convenience.
Amen.

PRAYER FOR TUESDAY:

Jesus,
Let Your teachings pierce my soul. Open my ears to truth. Show me where I need to grow in love, humility, and service.
Amen.

PRAYER FOR WEDNESDAY:

Father,
On this day when betrayal was set in motion, keep my heart stead-

fast. Help me choose loyalty over comfort, faith over fear.
Amen.

MAUNDY THURSDAY – A PRAYER ON THE LAST SUPPER AND CHRIST'S HUMILITY

SCRIPTURE:

"If I then, your Lord and Master, have washed your feet; ye also ought to wash one another's feet." – John 13:14 (KJV)

PRAYER:

Gracious Savior,
On this sacred night, You knelt before Your disciples and washed their feet. You broke bread and gave thanks, knowing the suffering that awaited You.
Teach me to serve others with humility and love. Let me never forget that greatness in Your kingdom comes through servanthood. Help me remember Your body and blood with reverence and awe.
Amen.

SCRIPTURE:

"But he was wounded for our transgressions, he was bruised for our iniquities..." – Isaiah 53:5 (KJV)

PRAYER:

Jesus,
Today I stand in silence at the foot of Your cross. My heart breaks as I remember the nails, the thorns, the suffering You bore for me. Thank You for Your love so fierce, so pure, so undeserved. Thank You for enduring the cross, despising its shame, that I might be forgiven and free.
Let me live a life worthy of such a gift.
Amen.

HOLY SATURDAY – A PRAYER OF WAITING AND HOPE IN THE SILENCE

SCRIPTURE:

"And they rested the sabbath day according to the commandment." – Luke 23:56 (KJV)

PRAYER:

Lord of the Waiting,
Today is quiet. The tomb is sealed. Hope seems hidden. And yet, I trust.
In the silence of this day, teach me to rest in You. Teach me to hope even when I do not see. Let my faith stretch beyond what is visible. I await the dawn, the stone rolled away, the victory You promised.
Amen.

SECTION 2: RESURRECTION

PRAYERS

Section 2:
Resurrection Prayers

Easter is the glorious
celebration of
the moment when sorrow turned to joy, despair to hope, and death
to life. These prayers are offered to help you reflect on the miracle
of the empty tomb, rejoice in the power of the risen Christ, and
carry the joy of Easter into your heart and your daily walk with Him.

Easter is the glorious celebration of Jesus' resurrection—the moment when sorrow turned to joy, despair to hope, and death to life. These prayers are offered to help you reflect on the miracle of the empty tomb, rejoice in the power of the risen Christ, and carry the joy of Easter into your heart and your daily walk with Him.

EASTER SUNDAY MORNING – A PRAYER OF REJOICING IN CHRIST'S VICTORY OVER DEATH

SCRIPTURE:

"He is not here: for he is risen, as he said." – Matthew 28:6 (KJV)

PRAYER:

Hallelujah!

Jesus, You are risen! The grave could not hold You, and death has been defeated.

This morning I rejoice with all creation. The stone is rolled away. Light has conquered darkness. Hope has been restored.

Let the joy of this day fill every corner of my heart. Let me live boldly in the power of Your resurrection. You are alive—and because of You, I live!

Amen.

PRAYER FOR NEW LIFE – EMBRACING THE RESURRECTION IN OUR HEARTS

SCRIPTURE:

"Therefore if any man be in Christ, he is a new creature: old things are passed away; behold, all things are become new." – 2 Corinthians 5:17 (KJV)

PRAYER:

Risen Lord,
Thank You for the gift of new life. Because You rose again, I am made new. Help me leave behind what is dead and broken, and walk in the freshness of Your grace.
Let the resurrection not be a one-day celebration, but a daily reality in my life. Renew my thoughts, my desires, my actions. Make me a reflection of Your living hope.
Amen.

PRAYER OF GRATITUDE FOR SALVATION – THANKING JESUS FOR HIS SACRIFICE

23

SCRIPTURE:

"But thanks be to God, which giveth us the victory through our Lord Jesus Christ." – 1 Corinthians 15:57 (KJV)

PRAYER:

Thank You, Jesus,
For going to the cross, for bearing my sin, for enduring the grave—and for rising again in glory.
I do not deserve such love, but I receive it with a heart full of gratitude.
Let my life be a continual offering of thanks. Let me never grow tired of praising You for the salvation You freely gave.
Amen.

PRAYER FOR STRENGTH IN FAITH – ASKING GOD TO DEEPEN OUR BELIEF IN CHRIST'S VICTORY

SCRIPTURE:

"Blessed are they that have not seen, and yet have believed." – John 20:29 (KJV)

PRAYER:

Lord,
Sometimes I doubt. Sometimes I struggle to see the truth when life is heavy.
But today, I cling to the power of the resurrection. Deepen my faith. Let my belief grow roots, strong and unshakable.
Even when I do not see, I will trust. Even when I do not feel, I will believe. You are risen—and You are with me.
Amen.

PRAYER OF HOPE AND RENEWAL – EMBRACING THE PROMISE OF ETERNAL LIFE

SCRIPTURE:

"Blessed be the God and Father of our Lord Jesus Christ… which hath begotten us again unto a lively hope by the resurrection of Jesus Christ from the dead." – 1 Peter 1:3 (KJV)

PRAYER:

Father of Hope,
In the resurrection of Christ, You have given me a reason to rejoice and a promise that cannot be shaken.
Let this Easter hope be alive in me, not just for today, but for all my days. Renew my spirit. Remind me that life eternal begins now—rooted in Your love and power.
Amen.

SECTION 3: EASTER WEEK & THE SEASON OF RESURRECTION

The joy of Easter is not confined to a single Sunday—it marks the beginning of a season that continute for weeks in the Christian calendar. During this time, we are invited to live in the light of the resurrection, to share the Good News boldly, and to **walk in faith** with renewed purpose.

These prayers are written to help you carry the miracle of Easter into your everyday life, drawing closer to God and growing. in hope.

The joy of Easter is not confined to a single Sunday—it marks the beginning of a season that continues for weeks in the Christian calendar. During this time, we are invited to live in the light of the resurrection, to share the Good News boldly, and to walk in faith with renewed purpose. These prayers are written to help you carry the miracle of Easter into your everyday life, drawing closer to God and growing in hope.

MONDAY AFTER EASTER – A PRAYER TO LIVE IN THE JOY OF THE RESURRECTION

SCRIPTURE:

"This is the day which the Lord hath made; we will rejoice and be glad in it." – Psalm 118:24 (KJV)

PRAYER:

Risen Lord,
As the first week of Easter unfolds, let not my joy fade with yesterday's celebration. You are still risen. The tomb is still empty.
Help me live in that joy—not just on Sunday, but on Monday, and every day that follows. May my face shine with resurrection light, and may my words bring hope to those around me.
Amen.

PRAYER FOR SHARING THE GOOD NEWS – ASKING FOR BOLDNESS TO SPREAD THE GOSPEL

SCRIPTURE:

"Go ye into all the world, and preach the gospel to every creature." – Mark 16:15 (KJV)

PRAYER:

Jesus,
You rose not just to redeem me, but to commission me. I am called to tell the world of Your victory.
Give me courage to speak. Give me love to serve. Give me wisdom to share Your story in ways that draw others to You.
Let my life be a living testimony of resurrection power.
Amen.

PRAYER FOR PEACE AND UNITY – FOLLOWING CHRIST'S EXAMPLE OF LOVE AND FORGIVENESS

SCRIPTURE:

"Peace be unto you: as my Father hath sent me, even so send I you." – John 20:21 (KJV)

PRAYER:

Prince of Peace,
You spoke peace to frightened hearts and offered forgiveness where there was failure.
Let Your peace reign in my relationships, my church, my home.
Heal divisions. Calm anxious hearts. Let the unity of Your Spirit bind us together in love.
Send me into the world as an agent of that peace.
Amen.

SCRIPTURE:

"Upon this rock I will build my church; and the gates of hell shall not prevail against it." – Matthew 16:18 (KJV)

PRAYER:

Lord of the Church,
Strengthen Your people. Renew our purpose. Ignite our worship.
Fill our leaders with wisdom, and our members with grace.
May we be a light in our communities, reflecting Your resurrection love to a hurting world.
Let us not grow weary in doing good, but continue to proclaim:
Christ is risen indeed!
Amen.

PRAYER FOR FAMILIES – INVITING JESUS INTO HOMES AND RELATIONSHIPS

SCRIPTURE:

"And if it seem evil unto you to serve the Lord… as for me and my house, we will serve the Lord." – Joshua 24:15 (KJV)

PRAYER:

Lord Jesus,
Come into our home and make it a place of peace, love, and joy.
Let our family celebrate Easter not just in church, but at the dinner table, in bedtime prayers, and in daily kindness.
Bind us together with love rooted in Your resurrection power. Let our home reflect Heaven.
Amen.

PRAYER FOR THOSE SEEKING FAITH – ASKING GOD TO REVEAL HIMSELF TO NEW BELIEVERS

SCRIPTURE:

"Seek, and ye shall find; knock, and it shall be opened unto you." – Matthew 7:7 (KJV)

PRAYER:

Father,
For all those searching, longing, and doubting—meet them where they are.
Show them the truth of the empty tomb. Let them feel Your love, hear Your voice, and know Your grace.
Draw new hearts to salvation. Let this Easter season be the beginning of many faith journeys.
Amen.

PRAYER FOR THE WORLD – PRAYING FOR RENEWAL AND HEALING THROUGH CHRIST

35

SCRIPTURE:

"For the earth shall be filled with the knowledge of the glory of the Lord, as the waters cover the sea." – Habakkuk 2:14 (KJV)

PRAYER:

Lord of all nations,
Our world is weary and broken. We need the healing only You can bring.
Let the resurrection power that conquered death now move across the earth—bringing justice where there is oppression, peace where there is war, and light where there is darkness.
Let Your glory cover the earth.
Amen.

SECTION 4: EASTER

REFLECTIONS AND BLESSINGS

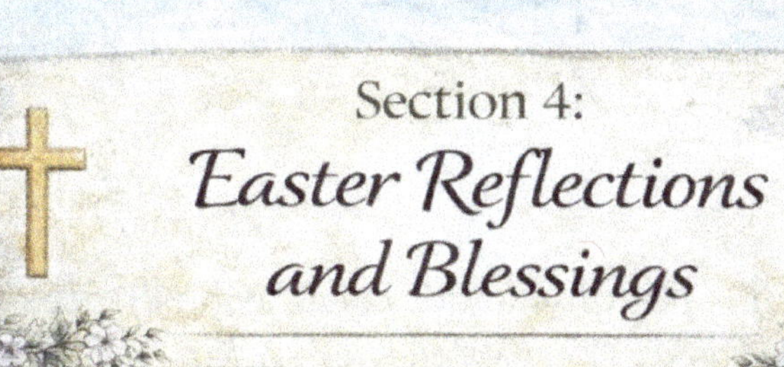

Section 4:
Easter Reflections and Blessings

The Easter season is not only about celebrating Christ's resurrection—it's about living it. These prayers are meant to carry the light of Easter into your daily rhythm, In the quiet of morning, in the stillness of night, and in moments of transition, may you return to the joy of Easter again and again.

Use these blessings and reflections to stay grounded in the hope. that lives within you.

The Easter season is not only about celebrating Christ's resurrection—it's about living it. These prayers are meant to carry the light of Easter into your daily rhythm. In the quiet of morning, in the stillness of night, and in moments of transition, may you return to the joy of Easter again and again. Use these blessings and reflections to stay grounded in the hope that lives within you.

MORNING EASTER BLESSING – STARTING EACH DAY IN RESURRECTION HOPE

SCRIPTURE:

"His compassions fail not. They are new every morning: great is thy faithfulness." – Lamentations 3:22–23 (KJV)

PRAYER:

Risen Lord,
With the rising sun, I remember that You are alive and at work in me.
Let today be filled with Your mercy and truth. May I greet this day with open hands and a grateful heart.
Let the resurrection power that brought You from the grave raise my spirit to live with purpose and joy.
This is a new day. I choose to walk in hope.
Amen.

EVENING PRAYER OF GRATITUDE – ENDING THE DAY WITH THANKSGIVING FOR EASTER JOY

SCRIPTURE:

"I will both lay me down in peace, and sleep: for thou, Lord, only makest me dwell in safety." – Psalm 4:8 (KJV)

PRAYER:

Father,
Thank You for this day, for every breath, every joy, every lesson.
As I lay down to rest, I release my worries to You. Remind me that the same power that raised Jesus lives in me.
Let peace guard my heart. Let praise linger on my lips.
Tonight, I sleep in the shelter of resurrection grace.
Amen.

PRAYER FOR SPIRITUAL GROWTH AFTER EASTER – CONTINUING TO WALK WITH CHRIST

SCRIPTURE:

"As ye have therefore received Christ Jesus the Lord, so walk ye in him."
– Colossians 2:6 (KJV)

PRAYER:

Lord Jesus,
Easter is not the end—it's a beginning. Help me walk in step with You beyond this season.
Deepen my roots in faith. Help me grow in love, in wisdom, in obedience.
May the joy of Easter be more than a feeling—it is the foundation of who I am becoming.
Guide me forward, one step at a time.
Amen.

PRAYER FOR PERSEVERANCE IN FAITH – HOLDING ONTO THE JOY OF THE RESURRECTION

SCRIPTURE:

"Let us not be weary in well doing: for in due season we shall reap, if we faint not." – Galatians 6:9 (KJV)

PRAYER:

Father,
When life grows hard or the days feel long, remind me of the empty tomb.
Help me hold on to the truth that Christ's victory is my hope—even when joy is hard to find.
Strengthen my faith. Steady my steps. Let the joy of Easter anchor me in every storm.
Amen.

PRAYER FOR ETERNAL LIFE – TRUSTING IN GOD'S PROMISE BEYOND THIS WORLD

SCRIPTURE:

"And this is the promise that he hath promised us, even eternal life." –
1 John 2:25 (KJV)

PRAYER:

Heavenly Father,
Because of Jesus, I do not fear the grave. You have given me the gift
of eternal life, and I trust Your promise.
Help me live each day with eternity in view—with peace, purpose,
and praise.
Let my heart long for Heaven, even as I serve faithfully here on
earth.
I believe in the resurrection. I believe in forever with You.
Amen.

SECTION 5: WEEKLY

DEVOTIONS

We deepen our faith by taking time for prayer, reflection and meditation on the life of Jesus.

In these weekly devotions, we well journey with our Lord through the desert of temptation, the streets of Jerusalem, the Upper Room, the Garden of Gethsemane, and ultimately, to Calvary.

Each weekly reflection includes a passage of Scripture and questions to guide your prayer and contemplation during Lent and Holy Week.

Weekly Devotional Reflections for Lent and Easter
accompany and deepen your prayer journey.

WEEK 1 – REPENTANCE & RETURN

SCRIPTURE:

"Turn ye even to me with all your heart, and with fasting, and with weeping, and with mourning." – Joel 2:12 (KJV)

DEVOTIONAL THOUGHT:

The season of Lent opens with a call to return to the Lord. This is not a superficial turning, but a deep surrender of heart, mind, and will. God's mercy is abundant, and repentance is not a punishment but an invitation to healing. The ashes on our forehead are a sign of both our frailty and God's faithful love.

REFLECTION QUESTION:

What do I need to surrender in order to return more fully to God this season?

WEEK 2 – WALKING IN HUMILITY

SCRIPTURE:

"He hath shewed thee... what doth the Lord require of thee, but to do justly, and to love mercy, and to walk humbly with thy God?" – Micah 6:8 (KJV)

DEVOTIONAL THOUGHT:

Jesus' journey to the cross was marked by humility. He served, healed, and forgave—never demanding, always giving. Lent is a chance to follow His example, to lower ourselves in pride so we might be raised up in grace.

REFLECTION QUESTION:

Where in my life is God calling me to choose humility over control or recognition?

WEEK 3 – ENDURING TEMPTATION

SCRIPTURE:

"For in that he himself hath suffered being tempted, he is able to succour them that are tempted." – Hebrews 2:18 (KJV)

DEVOTIONAL THOUGHT:

Jesus, though sinless, faced real temptation in the wilderness. He relied on the Word of God—not comfort or convenience. In our wilderness seasons, we are reminded that we do not face temptation alone. Christ walks with us, strengthens us, and gives us a way through.

REFLECTION QUESTION:

What temptations do I need to confront with truth and trust during this season?

WEEK 4 – EMBRACING THE CROSS

SCRIPTURE:

"And he bearing his cross went forth into a place called… Golgotha." – John 19:17 (KJV)

DEVOTIONAL THOUGHT:

The cross was not just Jesus' destiny—it is our call as disciples. To follow Christ means to carry our own cross: the hard things, the sacrifices, the faithful steps in the dark. When we embrace the cross, we also embrace the resurrection that follows.

REFLECTION QUESTION:

What "cross" is God asking me to carry with trust and obedience?

WEEK 5 – FORGIVENESS AND GRACE

SCRIPTURE:

"Father, forgive them; for they know not what they do." – Luke 23:34 (KJV)

DEVOTIONAL THOUGHT:

Even from the cross, Jesus offered forgiveness. As we approach Easter, we are challenged to release bitterness, extend mercy, and receive grace. Resurrection begins with forgiveness—both given and received.

REFLECTION QUESTION:

Who do I need to forgive so I can fully receive the joy of Easter?

WEEK 6 – AWAITING REDEMPTION (HOLY WEEK)

SCRIPTURE:

"Truly this was the Son of God." – Matthew 27:54 (KJV)

DEVOTIONAL THOUGHT:

Holy Week brings us to the edge of sorrow. From the cheers of Palm Sunday to the silence of Holy Saturday, we wait in tension. But even in the waiting, we are not alone. Redemption is coming. The cross was not the end—it was the doorway.

REFLECTION QUESTION:

How can I stay present with Christ this week, even in sorrow or silence?

WEEK 7 – RESURRECTION LIFE (EASTER WEEK)

SCRIPTURE:

"I am the resurrection, and the life: he that believeth in me, though he were dead, yet shall he live." – John 11:25 (KJV)

DEVOTIONAL THOUGHT:

Easter changes everything. It is not just about Jesus' rising—it's about our rising too. We are called to live with courage, to love without fear, and to move forward with eternal hope. The grave is empty. Our hearts are full.

REFLECTION QUESTION:

How will I live differently now because Christ is risen?

SECTION 6: FAMILY & CHILDREN'S PRAYERS

Section 6:
Family and Children's Prayers
Lent and Holy Week Prayers

Pray as a family in preparation for Easter.

Pray as a family in preparation for Easter.

- Explore child-friendly reflections for each week of Lent.

- Help children connect to the events of Holy Week as they prepare for the mystery and joy of Easter.

This chapter contains simple, heartfelt prayers to guide your family's Easter season.

The Easter story is for everyone—including the youngest hearts in our homes. This section offers short prayers and blessings written especially for children and families. Whether shared at the breakfast table, before bed, or during family devotions, these prayers invite children to celebrate the joy of Jesus' resurrection and feel God's love for them.

A CHILD'S PRAYER FOR EASTER MORNING

SCRIPTURE:

"Jesus said, Suffer little children, and forbid them not, to come unto me." – Matthew 19:14 (KJV)

PRAYER:

Dear Jesus,
Happy Easter! Thank You for rising from the dead.
You are alive forever, and I'm so glad You love me.
Help me to be kind, to forgive, and to share Your joy with others.
Thank You for being my forever friend.
Amen.

BEDTIME PRAYER DURING HOLY WEEK

PRAYER:

Dear God,
This week, I'm thinking about Jesus.
Thank You for His love. Thank You for the cross.
Help me remember that even when things seem sad,
Your love is stronger than anything.
I trust You, Lord.
Amen.

PRAYER:

Lord Jesus,
We gather at this table with grateful hearts.
Thank You for Your sacrifice, Your love, and the joy of Your resur-
rection.
Bless this food and everyone at this table.
May our hearts be full of faith, our voices full of praise,
and our lives full of Your light.
Amen.

A FAMILY PRAYER FOR THE WEEK AFTER EASTER

PRAYER:

God of New Life,
As we go through this week, let us carry Easter in our hearts.
Help us to walk in love, speak with kindness, and remember that
Jesus is always with us.
May our home be filled with joy, peace, and resurrection hope.
Amen.

PRAYER:

Jesus,
Sometimes I forget how much You love me.
But I know You died for me and rose again.
That means I'm never alone.
Thank You for being my Savior and my Friend.
Help me love You more every day.
Amen.

SECTION 7: EASTER BLESSINGS FOR SPECIAL OCCASIONS

Share blessings of hope, joy and encouragement
for your Easter gatherings and celebrations.

The resurrection of Jesus fills every corner of our lives with meaning—from quiet moments of personal faith to the joyful celebrations shared around a table or in a sanctuary. These blessings are crafted for special occasions during the Easter season. Use them at home, in church, or wherever hearts gather in the light of Christ's victory.

PRAYER:

Lord of Light,
As the sun rises, so does our hope.
We gather in awe of Your power, in gratitude for the cross,
and in wonder at the empty tomb.
Let this morning renew our hearts and awaken our faith.
May the light of Christ shine brighter than the sunrise,
and may we walk today—and always—in resurrection joy.
Amen.

PRAYER:

Heavenly Father,
Thank You for this table, for this food,
and for the hands that prepared it.
Most of all, thank You for Jesus—
for His death that gave us life, and His rising that gives us hope.
Bless our conversation, our laughter, our memories,
and our fellowship in You.
Christ is risen! He is risen indeed!
Amen.

PRAYER:

Risen Savior,
We rejoice in this step of faith.
Pour out Your Spirit on this beloved child of God.
Clothe them in grace, guide their steps in truth,
and surround them with the love of Your Church.
May their life always reflect the power of the resurrection,
and may they grow in faith, courage, and devotion to You.
Amen.

PRAYER:

Gracious God,
We thank You for the gift of family—of laughter, love, and belonging.
Help us to keep Easter alive in our home,
not just today but every day.
Fill our hearts with peace and our words with kindness.
Let forgiveness flow freely and joy dwell richly.
May the love that raised Jesus from the dead
fill our home with hope that never fades.
Amen.

A BLESSING FOR THOSE GRIEVING DURING EASTER

PRAYER:

Merciful Lord,
This Easter, some hearts are heavy.
While others rejoice, we grieve—and yet, we do not grieve without
hope.
Thank You for the promise that death is not the end.
Comfort those who mourn.
Hold them close with resurrection love.
Remind them that because Christ lives, we shall live also.
Amen.

SECTION 8: PERSONAL TESTIMONIES & SHORT STORIES

Section 8:
Personal Testimonies
Lent and Holy Week Prayers

Share how the Lenten and Holy Week journey has impacted your relationship with Jesus.

This Lenten season has allowed me to reflect deeply on Christ's sacrifice and love. It has drawn me closer to Him and transformed my heart.

David, California

Walking through Lent and Holy Week has been a time of renewed faith for me. I have experienced God's mercy and grace in a new and profound way.

Jessica, California

The following are Real stories of hope, healing, and Easter faith.

The resurrection of Jesus is not just a past event—it is a living hope that continues to transform hearts today. These brief testimonies offer glimpses of that transformation: moments of grace, answered prayers, and renewed faith, all made possible through the power of Christ.

"Easter was hard that year. My mother had passed just weeks before, and our family dinner table had an empty chair where she once sat. As we prayed before the meal, I quietly asked God to help me find peace. That evening, my youngest son—only six—stood up and said, 'Grandma's with Jesus now, and He's not dead anymore. So she's not really gone!' In that moment, God gave me what I needed: the simple, powerful truth of the resurrection."

REFLECTION:

Even in grief, Easter reminds us that death is not the end.

A SECOND CHANCE AT EASTER

"For years I drifted from my faith. Church was something I used to do, but it felt far away. Then one Palm Sunday, I accepted a neighbor's invitation to attend a small sunrise service. Something about that morning—the music, the sunrise, the story of Jesus riding into Jerusalem with full knowledge of the cross—broke me open. I wept. I prayed for the first time in years. And that Easter, I came home to God."

REFLECTION:

The path to Calvary is also the path back to grace.

THE RESURRECTION AND THE REHAB ROOM

"I was in recovery after a serious accident, and it was Easter Sunday. I couldn't move much, and I felt forgotten. But that morning, a volunteer came by and handed me a tiny Easter card with the words: *'He is risen. So will you.'* I don't know who wrote it, but I wept. It gave me strength. I pinned it beside my bed, and every time I looked at it, I believed a little more."

REFLECTION:

Resurrection hope reaches even the loneliest rooms.

LILY'S FIRST PRAYER

"Our daughter, Lily, was only four when she heard the Easter story in Sunday School. That night, she asked if Jesus was 'still alive.' I told her yes, and she whispered, 'Then I want to talk to Him.' She closed her eyes and prayed, 'Hi Jesus. Thank You for not staying dead. I love You.' That was her first real prayer. I cried. And I knew: Easter had already taken root in her heart."

REFLECTION:

Even the smallest voices can carry resurrection faith.

"In a prison chapel, surrounded by men from every background, I witnessed something I'll never forget: a simple wooden cross, a cracked guitar, and voices rising with the words, *'Because He lives, I can face tomorrow.'*

That Easter, I realized that no wall, no sin, no failure could keep the risen Christ from reaching us. We weren't just inmates—we were forgiven, and free in Him."

REFLECTION:

The resurrection breaks chains—seen and unseen.

A MOTHER'S EASTER PRAYER ANSWERED

"As a single mom, Easter always brought both joy and exhaustion. I wanted it to be special for my kids, but money was tight, and my heart felt worn. That year, I quietly prayed, 'Lord, let my children feel Your love.'

Later that morning, a neighbor brought over an Easter basket filled with goodies—with a card that simply said, *'He sees you. He loves you.'* I cried in the kitchen. It wasn't just a kind gesture—it was an answer to prayer. My kids saw Jesus that day, and so did I."

REFLECTION:

God often meets us in quiet desperation—with gentle miracles.

A LITTLE GIRL'S EASTER OFFERING

"My daughter, Anna, was five when she brought me her piggy bank during Lent. She said, 'I want Jesus to have this because He gave everything for me.' I asked what she meant, and she said, 'He gave His life, so I can give my coins.'

We brought it to church and gave it to the children's mission fund on Easter Sunday. She placed it in the basket with both hands and smiled so big. I've never forgotten that moment—pure faith wrapped in a child's heart."

REFLECTION:

Even the smallest offerings become holy in the hands of a child.

"After escaping an abusive marriage, I found myself at a women's shelter with nothing but a few clothes and a bruised spirit. It was Holy Saturday. I had no plans for Easter. But the next morning, a volunteer brought a simple breakfast, and we held hands and prayed.

She reminded us that the stone was rolled away—and that we could rise, too. That was the first day I began to believe in healing. Not just survival. Healing. Resurrection wasn't just for Jesus. It was for me, too."

REFLECTION:

Easter hope breaks through even the darkest seasons.

A DAUGHTER'S LETTER TO JESUS

"My 8-year-old wrote a letter one Holy Week and left it on her windowsill. It read: *'Dear Jesus, I love You more than chocolate. I know You love me even when I mess up. Thank You for dying and coming back alive. I want to be with You forever.'*

She didn't tell me she wrote it. I found it later that night—and it brought me to tears. She didn't just know the Easter story. She believed it."

REFLECTION:

Sometimes the purest theology is written in crayon.

SECTION 9: EASTER SYMBOLS, TRADITIONS & REFLECTIONS

Section 9:
Easter Symbols, Traditions, and Reflections
Lent and Holy Week Prayers

Learn the deeper meaning and significance of Easter symbols and customs, and reflect on the timeless traditions of Lent and Holy Week.

Discovering the sacred meaning behind the signs of the season
can be an important step.

The Easter season is rich with visual and spiritual symbolism.
From lilies and lambs to empty tombs and bright sunrise services,
each tradition points to the deeper truth of Christ's death and resurrection. This section explores the meaning behind some of the
most beloved Easter elements, offering Scripture and reflection to
help you see them with fresh eyes and renewed wonder.

THE CROSS – A SYMBOL OF SACRIFICE AND VICTORY

The cross, once a symbol of death, has become the centerpiece of our faith. It reminds us that Jesus bore our sins and triumphed over darkness.

SCRIPTURE:

"But God forbid that I should glory, save in the cross of our Lord Jesus Christ." – Galatians 6:14 (KJV)

REFLECTION:

When you see the cross, do you see sorrow or victory? How does Christ's sacrifice change the way you live today?

THE EMPTY TOMB – A SIGN OF HOPE

The stone was rolled away not so Jesus could escape—but so we could see that He is risen. The empty tomb reminds us that nothing, not even death, can separate us from God's love.

SCRIPTURE:

"He is not here: for he is risen." – Matthew 28:6 (KJV)

REFLECTION:

What does the empty tomb mean for your fears, your doubts, and your future?

EASTER LILIES – PURITY AND RESURRECTION

White lilies often decorate churches and homes during Easter. Their trumpet shape announces the good news of Christ's victory, while their white petals symbolize purity and new life.

SCRIPTURE:

"Consider the lilies of the field, how they grow." – Matthew 6:28 (KJV)

REFLECTION:

When you see Easter lilies bloom, what do they say to your soul about growth, beauty, and new beginnings?

SUNRISE SERVICES – LIGHT BREAKING THROUGH DARKNESS

Many Christians gather at sunrise on Easter morning to remember the dawn when Christ rose. The first light of day is a powerful picture of resurrection.

SCRIPTURE:

"And very early in the morning... they came unto the sepulchre at the rising of the sun." – Mark 16:2 (KJV)

REFLECTION:

Where in your life are you waiting for light to break through? How can you begin your mornings with resurrection hope?

THE LAMB – CHRIST OUR SACRIFICE

Jesus is called the Lamb of God, a title rooted in the Old Testament Passover. His death is the ultimate and final sacrifice that takes away our sin.

SCRIPTURE:

"Behold the Lamb of God, which taketh away the sin of the world." – John 1:29 (KJV)

REFLECTION:

Do you approach God with gratitude for what Jesus has done as your Passover Lamb?

EGGS & NEW LIFE – A MODERN SYMBOL OF RESURRECTION

Though not directly biblical, the egg has long been a symbol of new life. In Christian tradition, it reflects the sealed tomb from which life broke forth. Decorating and hunting for eggs can be made sacred with the right heart.

SCRIPTURE:

"If any man be in Christ, he is a new creature." – 2 Corinthians 5:17 (KJV)

REFLECTION:

How can you use everyday traditions like egg decorating or gift-giving to point your family to the deeper truth of Easter?

SECTION 10: FAMILY

DEVOTIONS AND ACTIVITIES

Section 10:
Family Devotions and Activities
Lent and Holy Week Prayers

Explore ways for families to draw closer to God and celebrate the season together.

Explore ways for families to draw closer to God and celebrate the season together.

The Easter season provides a powerful opportunity to disciple children, deepen family faith, and build holy traditions that will last a lifetime. These short, simple devotions and activities are perfect for busy families who want to create space for Jesus in the days surrounding Easter.

Each devotion includes a scripture, a thought or question, and a suggested activity to bring it to life.

DEVOTION 1: THE LIGHT OF EASTER MORNING

SCRIPTURE:

"He is not here: for he is risen." – Matthew 28:6 (KJV)

TALK ABOUT IT:

What does it mean that Jesus is alive today?

ACTIVITY:

- Light a candle at breakfast on Easter morning.
- Say, "This light reminds us that Jesus is alive!"
- Each family member can share one thing they're thankful for.

DEVOTION 2: ROLLING AWAY THE STONE

SCRIPTURE:

"The stone was rolled away from the sepulchre." – Luke 24:2 (KJV)

TALK ABOUT IT:

What does the empty tomb tell us about God's power?

ACTIVITY:

- Find a small stone for each family member.
- Write a fear or burden on it with a washable marker.
- Roll them away together as you say, "He is risen!"

DEVOTION 3: SHARING THE GOOD NEWS

SCRIPTURE:

"Go... and tell his disciples that he is risen from the dead." – Matthew 28:7 (KJV)

TALK ABOUT IT:

Who can we tell about Jesus today?

ACTIVITY:

- Create Easter cards or artwork together and deliver to neighbors, friends, or church members.

- Include a simple message like "Jesus loves you" or "Happy Easter—He is Risen!"

DEVOTION 4: SIGNS OF NEW LIFE

SCRIPTURE:

"If any man be in Christ, he is a new creature." – 2 Corinthians 5:17 (KJV)

TALK ABOUT IT:

What is something God is growing or changing in you?

ACTIVITY:

- Plant a flower seed in a small pot or cup.
- Water it and place it in the sun.
- As it grows, talk about how God grows us, too.

DEVOTION 5: THE JOY OF RESURRECTION

SCRIPTURE:

"Rejoice in the Lord always." – Philippians 4:4 (KJV)

TALK ABOUT IT:

What makes Easter joyful? How can we celebrate?

ACTIVITY:

- Create a "Joy Jar"—each family member writes one joyful moment from the week and puts it in the jar.
- Read them aloud on Sunday to celebrate God's goodness.

SECTION 11: JOURNAL

PAGES & REFLECTIONS

Section 11:
Journal Pages and Reflections
Lent and Holy Week Prayers

Deepen your prayer experience through journaling pages for writing reflections, prayer requests, and insights as you journey through Lent and Holy Week.

- Remain focused during Lent

- Record inspirations and prayers.

Write your way into deeper faith this Easter season.

Journaling is a sacred practice. It helps us slow down, pay attention, and open our hearts more fully to God. During the Easter season, we are invited not only to remember what Christ has done but also to ask what He is doing in us right now. This section offers guided prompts to reflect on themes of repentance, renewal, resurrection, and rejoicing—one for each week from Ash Wednesday through Easter.

WEEK 1 – ASH WEDNESDAY & THE START OF LENT

VERSE:

"Create in me a clean heart, O God…" – Psalm 51:10

PROMPT:

What do I need to surrender at the start of this journey?

GRATITUDE TODAY:

WEEK 2 – REPENTANCE & RETURN

VERSE:

"Turn ye even to me with all your heart..." – Joel 2:12

PROMPT:

Where is God inviting me to return to Him more fully?

GRATITUDE TODAY:

VERSE:

"Walk humbly with thy God." – Micah 6:8

PROMPT:

How can I practice humility in my relationships this week?

GRATITUDE TODAY:

WEEK 4 – ENDURING TEMPTATION

VERSE:

"He is able to succour them that are tempted." – Hebrews 2:18

PROMPT:

What temptations do I need strength to overcome?

GRATITUDE TODAY:

WEEK 5 – EMBRACING THE CROSS

VERSE:

"Let him deny himself, and take up his cross daily..." – Luke 9:23

PROMPT:

What does "taking up my cross" look like in my life?

GRATITUDE TODAY:

WEEK 6 – WAITING IN THE DARK (HOLY WEEK)

VERSE:

"They rested… according to the commandment." – Luke 23:56

PROMPT:

How do I respond when I'm asked to wait in faith?

GRATITUDE TODAY:

VERSE:

"If any man be in Christ, he is a new creature." – 2 Corinthians 5:17

PROMPT:

What new life is God creating in me this Easter?

GRATITUDE TODAY:

BONUS SECTIONS

SCRIPTURE CHART

LENTEN & EASTER SCRIPTURE READING PLAN — CHECK-OFF CHART

Day	Date	Old Testament Passage	✔	New Testament Passage	✔
Ash Wed		Joel 2:12–17		Matthew 6:1–6, 16–21	
Day 2		Psalm 51		Romans 12:1–2	
Day 3		Isaiah 58:1–12		James 1:19–27	
Day 4		Deuteronomy 30:15–20		Luke 9:23–27	
Day 5		Exodus 3:1–12		Matthew 4:18–22	
Day 6		Isaiah 6:1–8		Mark 8:34–38	
Day 7		1 Samuel 3:1–10		John 1:35–51	
Day 8		Jeremiah 1:4–10		Matthew 10:16–33	
Day 9		Psalm 25		Luke 14:25–33	
Day 10		Proverbs 3:1–8		Philippians 3:7–14	
Day 11		Genesis 3:1–19		Matthew 4:1–11	
Day 12		Psalm 91		1 Corinthians 10:12–13	
Day 13		Job 1:6–22		Hebrews 2:14–18	
Day 14		Isaiah 43:1–7		Romans 8:31–39	
Day 15		Psalm 46		Matthew 6:25–34	
Day 16		Psalm 119:105–112		John 16:33	

Day 17	Isaiah 50:4–10	Mark 10:32–45
Day 18	Psalm 22:1–21	Matthew 16:21–28
Day 19	Zechariah 12:10–13:1	Luke 18:31–43
Day 20	Lamentations 3:19–33	2 Corinthians 4:7–18
Day 21	Exodus 12:1–30	John 1:29–34
Day 22	Genesis 22:1–14	Romans 5:6–11
Day 23	Micah 7:18–20	Colossians 3:12–17
Day 24	Isaiah 1:16–20	Matthew 18:21–35
Day 25	Psalm 103:1–14	Ephesians 4:31–5:2
Day 26	Hosea 6:1–6	Luke 15:11–32
Day 27	Psalm 32	1 John 1:5–10
Day 28	Isaiah 53:1–6	John 3:14–21
Palm Sun	Zechariah 9:9–13	Matthew 21:1–11
Mon	Isaiah 42:1–9	Matthew 21:12–22
Tue	Isaiah 49:1–7	Matthew 21:23–46
Wed	Isaiah 50:4–9	Matthew 26:1–16
Maundy Thu	Exodus 12:43–51	John 13:1–17
Good Fri	Isaiah 52:13–53:12	John 18–19
Holy Sat	Lamentations 3:1–33	Matthew 27:57–66
Easter	Psalm 118:14–24	John 20:1–18

EASTER BLESSING CARDS

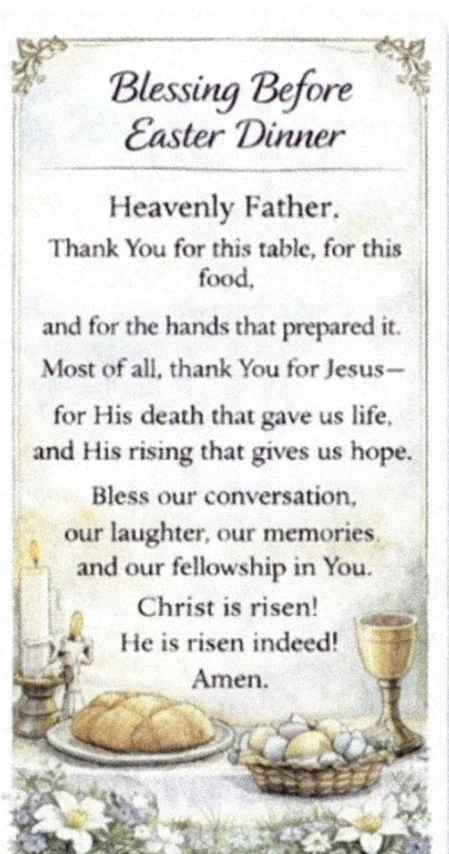

Blessing Before
Easter Dinner

Heavenly Father,
Thank You for this table, for this
food,

and for the hands that prepared it.

Most of all, thank You for Jesus—

for His death that gave us life,
and His rising that gives us hope.

Bless our conversation,
our laughter, our memories,
and our fellowship in You.

Christ is risen!
He is risen indeed!
Amen.

Blessing for
Families on Easter Sunday

Gracious God,
We thank You for the gift of family—
of laughter, love, and belonging.

Help us to keep Easter alive in our
home.
not just today but every day.

Fill our hearts with peace and
our words with kindness.

Let forgivenes flow freely
and joy dwell richly.

Amen.

A Blessing for Those Grieving During Easter

Merciful Lord,
This Easter, some hearts are heavy.

While others rejoice, we grieve—
and yet, we do not grieve without hope.

Thank You for the promise that
death is not the end.
Comfort those who mourn.

Hold them close with resurrection love.
Remind them that because Christ
lives, we shall live also.

Amen.

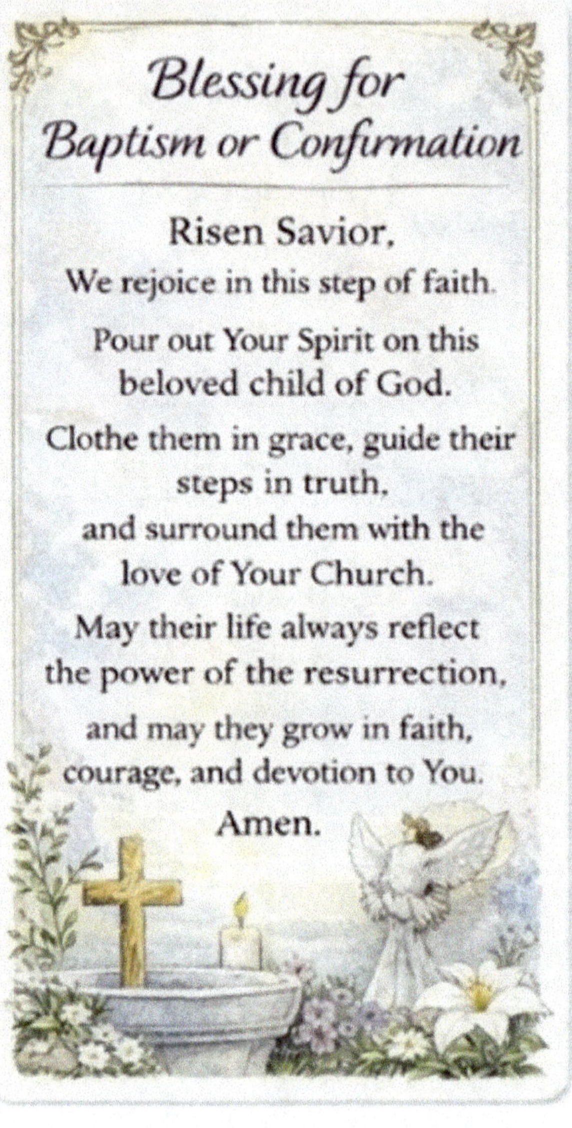

Blessing for
Baptism or Confirmation

Risen Savior,
We rejoice in this step of faith.

Pour out Your Spirit on this
beloved child of God.

Clothe them in grace, guide their
steps in truth,
and surround them with the
love of Your Church.

May their life always reflect
the power of the resurrection,

and may they grow in faith,
courage, and devotion to You.

Amen.

PRAYER CARDS

A Prayer
Before Easter Dinner

Lord Jesus,
We gather at this *table with* grateful
hearts. Thank You for Your
sacrifice, Your love,
and the joy of your resurrection.

Bless this food and everyone
at this table.
May our hearts be fulll of faith,
our voices full of praise,
and our lives full of Your light.

Amen.

Bedtime Prayer
During Holy Week

Dear God,
This week, I'm thinking about Jesus.

Thank You for His love.
Thank You for the cross.

Help me remember that even when
things seem sad,

Your love is stronger
than anything.

I trust You, Lord.

Amen.

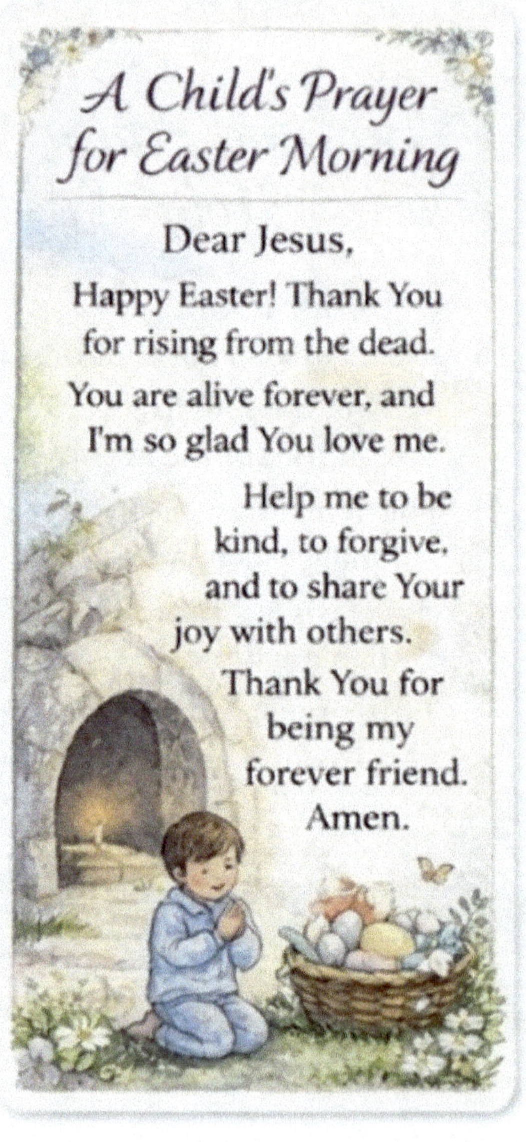

A Child's Prayer
for Easter Morning

Dear Jesus,
Happy Easter! Thank You
for rising from the dead.
You are alive forever, and
I'm so glad You love me.
Help me to be
kind, to forgive,
and to share Your
joy with others.
Thank You for
being my
forever friend.
Amen.

A Family Prayer
for the Week After Easter

God of New Life,
As we go through this week, let us
carry Easter in our hearts.
Help us to walk in love,
speak with kindness,
and remember that Jesus
is always with us.

May our home be filled
with joy, peace, and
resurrection hope.
Amen.

A Prayer to Know Jesus' Love

Jesus.
Sometimes I forget
how much You love me.

But I know You died
for me and rose again.

That means I'm never alone.

Thank You for being
my Savior and my Friend.

Help me love You more
every day.
Amen.

COLORING PAGES

The Cross

Galatians 6:14

But God forbid that I should glory, save in the cross of our Lord Jesus Christ.

Eggs & New Life

2 Corinthians 5:12

If any man be in Christ, he is a new creature.

The Empty Tomb

Matthew 28:6

He is not here: for He is risen.

Easter Lilies

Matthew 6:28

Consider the lilies of the field, which they grow.

Sunrise Services

Mark 16:2

And very early in the morning... they came unto the sepulchre at the rising of the sun.

ABOUT THE AUTHOR

Karen Kazimer Shockley

Karen Kazimer Shockley is a passionate author who has touched the hearts of readers with her inspiring books centered on celebrating holidays, heartfelt romances, and uplifting stories about Christianity.

Her works beautifully weave together faith, love, and the joy of special moments, creating stories that resonate with readers of all ages.

GRACE FOR EVERY SEASON

Discover the perfect companion for celebrating life's most meaningful moments with Grace for Every Season, a heartfelt series dedicated to bringing faith and inspiration to special occasions. Whether it's the joy of a wedding day, the solemnity of a memorial service, or the warmth of a holiday gathering, this series combines thoughtfully selected Bible verses, reflective insights, and soul-stirring prayers to honor every event.

Each volume is tailored to specific themes, including milestones, holidays, and seasons of life, ensuring a message of hope and encouragement is always close at hand. From uplifting passages to guide new beginnings, to gentle reminders of God's love during challenging times, Grace for Every Season is a celebration of His presence in all moments, big and small.

Perfect for personal devotion, group prayer, or as a gift to share with others, this series offers timeless wisdom and spiritual guidance to inspire hearts and unite communities. With its thoughtful blend of scripture, reflection, and prayer, Grace for Every Season invites readers to experience God's grace anew, whenever and wherever life unfolds.

God's Design For Her

Find Strength, Grace, and Encouragement—One Week at a Time

Life is busy, but your faith journey matters. God's Design For Her: 52 Bible Verses for Women is a year-long devotional designed to uplift and inspire you. Each week, you'll find a carefully chosen

Bible verse, a thoughtful reflection, and a heartfelt prayer—all created to help you grow in faith, embrace your God-given purpose, and walk confidently in His love.

Whether you're seeking peace, wisdom, or encouragement, this book will remind you that you are cherished, strong, and never alone. Take a few moments each week to draw closer to God and discover the beauty of His promises for you.

Start your journey today—because His grace is with you, every step of the way.

Not Just January: 52 Weekly Devotions To Begin Today

Begin your year—any time of the year—with the timeless truths of God's Word.

Experience a full year of encouragement, one week at a time, through 52 handpicked verses from the King James Bible—each one beautifully paired with reflections that invite you into deeper faith, renewed hope, abiding love, and joyful celebration.

Whether you're beginning in January or starting fresh in June, this devotional is designed with flexibility in mind. Each weekly entry features:

A powerful Bible verse from the beloved King James Version

An uplifting reflection to help you connect the verse to your daily life

A spiritual focus—Faith, Hope, Love, or Celebration—to guide your week

Encouragement and application to draw you closer to God

Perfect for morning devotionals, weekly quiet time, or as a thoughtful gift for a friend, this book will become a cherished companion on your walk with the Lord.

No matter the day or season, there's always time to grow your faith. Let this devotional remind you: You can start today.

Easter Devotional: 40 Days Of Verses And Prayers For Lent

Welcome to Easter Devotionals—your companion on a powerful, faith-filled journey toward the joyous celebration of Easter!

This book is more than just a guide; it's an invitation to walk closely with Christ through the season of Lent and beyond. Each page is designed to uplift your spirit, challenge your heart, and draw you deeper into the love and redemption found in Jesus.

A Journey of Transformation
As we embark on this sacred path together, my prayer is that Easter Devotionals ignites a fresh sense of hope, renewal, and faith within you. Here's what you can expect along the way:

Daily Scripture Readings – Immerse yourself in hand-selected Bible passages that reflect the themes of repentance, renewal, and redemption. These verses are meant to encourage and inspire as you meditate on God's Word and its profound impact on your life.

Heartfelt Prayers – Each day includes a prayer designed to strengthen your connection with God. Use them as a starting point to pour out your heart—whether in gratitude, surrender, or seeking His guidance.

Meaningful Insights – Alongside the scriptures, you'll find reflections that bring deeper understanding to the verses.
These interpretations will help bridge the ancient wisdom of the Bible with the realities of your daily walk of faith.

Community & Reflection – Faith grows when shared! Consider journeying through this devotional with a small group, your family, or an online community. Engage in meaningful discussions, share insights, and lift one another up in prayer.

Living Your Faith – Easter is not just a moment; it's a transformation! Allow the truths you uncover in these pages to shape your thoughts, words, and actions—bringing the light of Christ into every corner of your life.
Are you ready to embark on this soul-stirring journey? Let's dive in with open hearts, expectant faith, and a deep desire to draw closer to our risen Savior!

Angelic Reflections

Embrace a year of divine inspiration with Angelic Reflections: 52 Bible Verses and Prayers. This enriching book presents a curated selection of 52 powerful Bible verses that celebrate the presence and protection of angels in our lives. Each verse is paired with thoughtful interpretations that illuminate its meaning, guiding you to a deeper understanding of God's promises.

Accompanying each reflection is a heartfelt prayer designed to help you invite angelic blessings into your daily life. These prayers serve as a tool for connection, offering encouragement and peace as you navigate the joys and challenges of the year ahead.

Whether you're seeking strength, comfort, or guidance, Angelic Reflections: 52 Bible Verses and Prayers will be your companion on this spiritual journey. Each week, take a moment to reflect on the scriptures, meditate on their meanings, and lift your heart in prayer. Allow the wisdom of God's word to guide you, uplift your spirit, and fill your days with hope and gratitude.

Start your New Year with intention, faith, and the heavenly assurance that you are never alone. Let Angelic Blessings be your source of light and inspiration as you embrace a year of abundant blessings and divine protection!

New Year, New You

A Year of Faith, Hope, Love, and Celebration – One Verse at a Time!

Immerse yourself in a year of biblical inspiration with this beautifully curated devotional featuring 52 verses from the King James Bible—one for each week of the year. Designed to uplift, encourage, and guide you through every season, this book provides a refreshing way to deepen your faith and draw closer to God.

Each verse is thoughtfully organized into four key themes:

Faith – Strengthen your trust in God's promises.
Hope – Find reassurance in His never-ending grace.
Love – Experience the depth of His unconditional love.
Celebration – Rejoice in the goodness and joy of the Lord.

More than just a collection of verses, this devotional includes meaningful reflections and practical applications to help you live out God's Word in your daily life. Whether you're looking for encouragement, spiritual renewal, or a deeper understanding of Scripture, this book will be a source of strength and joy throughout the year.

Let the power of Scripture inspire your journey—one week at a time! Perfect for personal devotion, group study, or as a heartfelt gift for friends and family.